This Book Belongs To: _____

Parent(s) Name: _____

My Birthday: _____

Place of Birth: _____ **Time:** _____

Color at birth Eyes:_____ Hair:_____ Weight: _____

Length:_____ First word:_____

Paternal Grandparents: _____

Maternal Grandparents: _____

Siblings: _____

_____

connections
of L♡VE

Family Orgin/History: _____

_____

_____

Parent and Child Gift of Life's Journey

Keepsake Book

Love Letters and Talking Points for Parents and Children

Author: Sharon Nguyen, MA
Illustrations By, Sharon Nguyen and Sue Hartmann

Parent and Child Gift of Life's Journey
Title ID: 5585085
Universal ISBN-13: 978-0692479469

www.EmbraceGrace.net

This Book is written with all my love to my daughter. My darling daughter, I want you to always know how much I love you, even before you in my womb. I have always wanted a family and children, since I was a little girl. No matter how hard life was, I wanted someone to call my own and look forward to coming home to a beautiful face like yours. I cannot wait to see where life will lead you. If it happens to be that somehow I cannot be with you along the way, I want you to have this book to help you celebrate the good and bad times of life. I will always be in your heart and helping your guardian angels to protect you.

I want to say that I am sorry that you did not have two parent at birth, though I hope that I have and continue to give you ten times the amount of love, hugs and kisses, in addition to some discipline. My dreams and hopes for you are to live with compassion and to be passionate in all that you do. Live well and stand up for what you believe in and serve others. I hope that you will love school, as much as I did and achieve the highest level of education that you can reach. Do the best that you can do and have fun. I want to let you to know that you are a gift from God and my angel in disguise.

Love always, Mama

We want to give special thanks to my Godparents for assisting with editing and illustrations, my Godmother Sue Hartmann and my late Godfather Ed Hartmann. May he RIP.

Dear Parent Readers,

We are all Mothers and Fathers regardless of our gender. Parent involvement makes big impact in a child's life. This book is written to help parents and children to better understand different developmental stages, celebrate significant lives achievements and create parent-child opportunities for bonding and reflection. This book is to help parents and children to talk about topics open and honestly.

Each page has a space to journal your thoughts and feelings together. On the back side of each page is space to make your own personal page. Stick your favorite photo or draw a picture and write down your own life's event. I'm sure that this will be treasured at any age, where might a parent's departure may be sooner, than later. Happy Endings.

75% of the book proceeds will go towards strengthing Embrace Grace into a nonprofit organization. Supporting Social Equality for all.

Embrace Grace

Support Social Equality

www.embracegrace.net

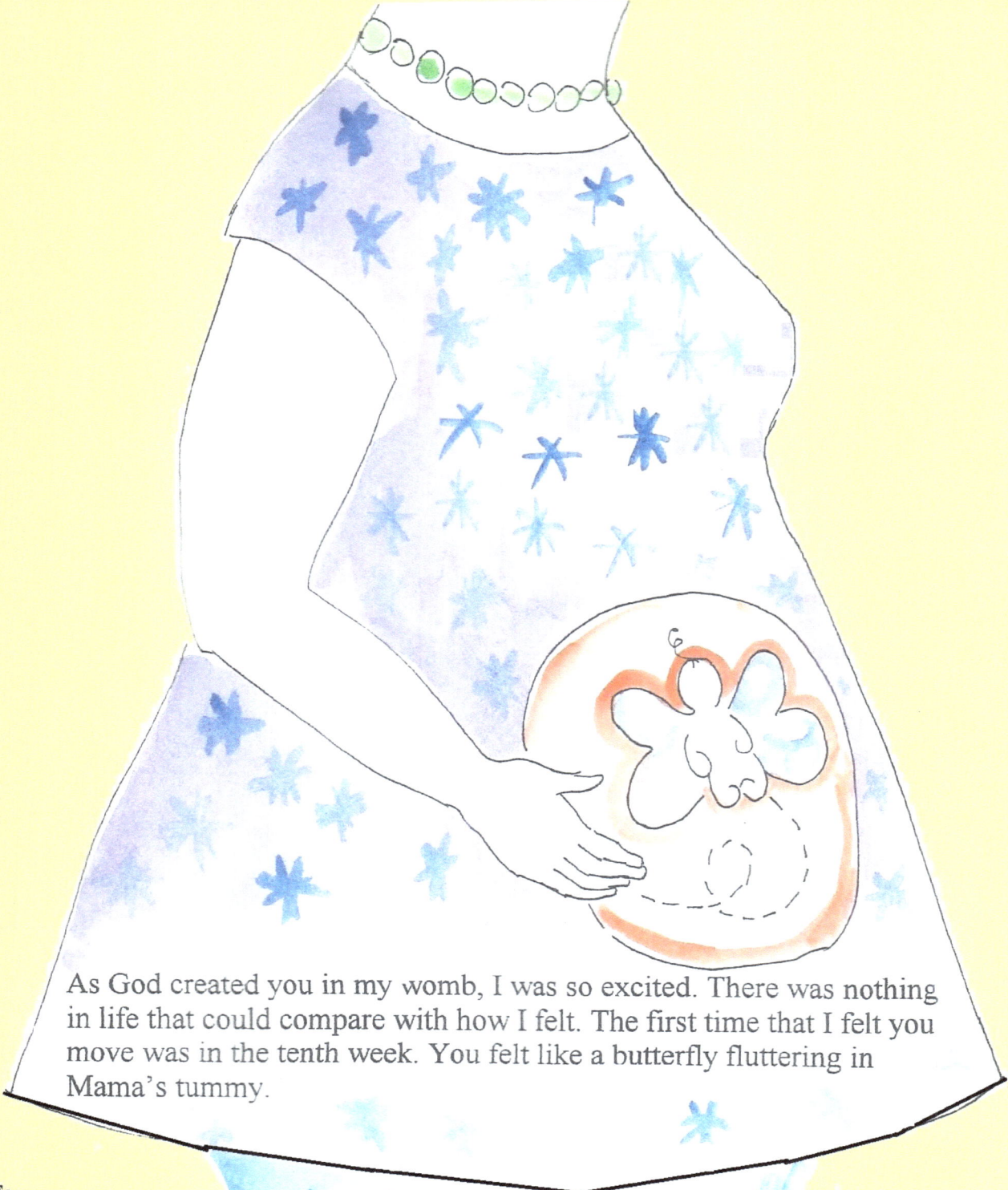

As God created you in my womb, I was so excited. There was nothing in life that could compare with how I felt. The first time that I felt you move was in the tenth week. You felt like a butterfly fluttering in Mama's tummy.

DATE: _____

JOURNAL: _____
_____
_____
_____
_____

Our Special Moments

Date: _____ Time: _____ Location: _____

Journal: _____

_____

_____

_____

_____

_____

_____

_____

_____

_____

_____

_____

My heart beats
for you my Love!

WEE WEE

As the weeks and months went by, I felt you kicking, tumbling and moving your back against my tummy. One of the best things was to hear your heart each time I went to the doctor.

DATE: _____

JOURNAL: _____
_____
_____
_____

Our Special Moments

Date: _____ **Time:** _____ **Location:** _____

Journal: _____

_____

_____

_____

_____

_____

_____

_____

_____

_____

_____

_____

JOY TO THE WORLD!

Happy Birthday!

I remembered for the first time I saw you, as I awoke from the medicine; my blurred eyes saw your beautiful face, and my ears heard your cries. We welcomed you into the world with joy, and I sang HAPPY BIRTHDAY to you, in my heart. We all felt a bundle of joy. We have many hopes and dreams for you, in the years to come.

DATE: _____

JOURNAL: _____

_____

_____

_____

_____

Our Special Moments

Date: _____ **Time:** _____ **Location:** _____

Journal: _____

_____

_____

_____

_____

_____

_____

_____

_____

_____

_____

I felt how much you love me, as you moved your body like an inch worm on my chest to eat. Then you moved yourself up to give me a kiss on the lips. I will never forget this image; it will be with me forever. Oh, how much I love you. I can't wait to do many things with you.

DATE: _____

JOURNAL: _____
_____
_____
_____
_____

Our Special Moments

Date: _____ **Time:** _____ **Location:** _____

Journal: _____

_____

_____

_____

_____

_____

_____

_____

_____

_____

_____

I'M #1 NOW

I'm so amazed with your first year of life. Sitting, crawling, standing, walking, laughing and saying your first word, filled me with joy. I have prepared and made plans for you as much as possible, so that you will not have to make hard decisions. I love you so much.

DATE: _____

JOURNAL: _____

_____

_____

_____

_____

Our Special Moments

Date: _____ **Time:** _____ **Location:** _____

Journal: _____

_____

_____

_____

_____

_____

_____

_____

_____

_____

_____

_____

HIP HIP HURRAY

GOOD JOB!

plop plop

DRIZZLE DRIZZLE

At two to three years old, it's time for you to practice potty training. As soon as you drizzle and make plop sounds in the toilet, I have a special gift for you. Job well done, you can potty in the toilet. Hip Hip Hurray!!!

DATE: _____

JOURNAL: _____

_____

_____

_____

_____

_____

Our Special Moments

Date: _____ **Time:** _____ **Location:** _____

Journal: _____

_____

_____

_____

_____

_____

_____

_____

_____

_____

_____

_____

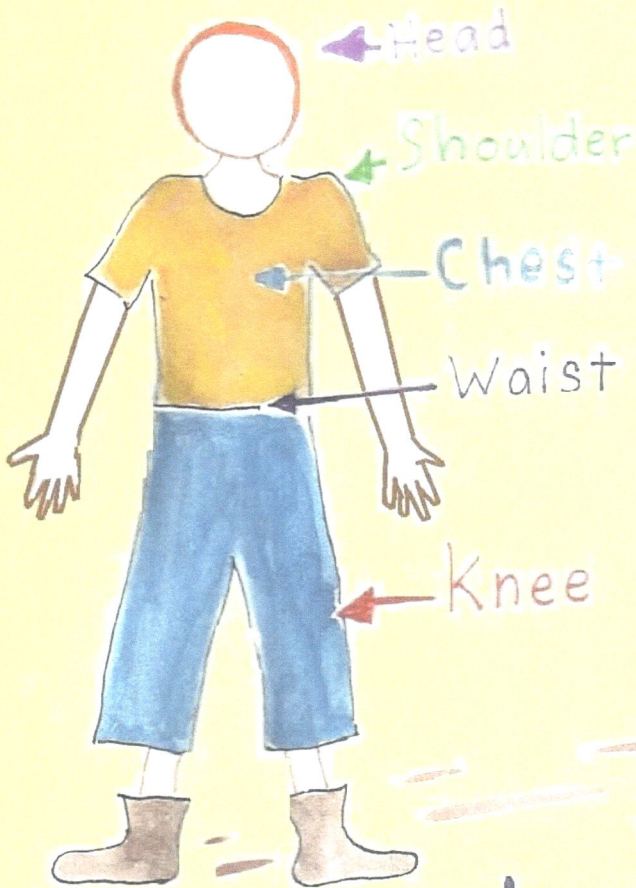

Head
Shoulder
Chest
Waist
Knee

My body parts to keep safe from my chest to my knees.

BE STRONG! - SAY NO! NO!

My Love, now that you how to go potty in the toilet and understand some of your body parts. I want to tell you that the body parts that you pee and poop are your special areas, even though; it may seem yucky. You may even be curious about your body parts yourself. Do not let anyone touch your special areas. If someone does or tells you to keep a secret, don't be afraid to say "No, I don't keep secrets!" Tell your Mom, Dad or someone you feel save with. You will read this page often to help you remember. I love you Sweet Pea.

DATE: _____

JOURNAL: _____

_____

_____

_____

_____

TELL SOMEONE

Our Special Moments

Date: _____   **Time:** _____   **Location:** _____

Journal: _____

_____

_____

_____

_____

_____

_____

_____

_____

_____

_____

_____

THE SECRET
CODE WORD

_ _ _ ? _ _

OK

We have a secret code that only people who can take you places will know. Even when you might know a person, such as a friend's parent, they need to know the code word, before you go with them. When you don't know someone and they ask you to go with them or to help them find their lost puppy, ask for the secret code. If the person cannot give you the code, run the other way and tell someone you feel safe with for help. Not all people are good, and you don't need to say Hi or talk to someone that you don't know. Safety first, my love.

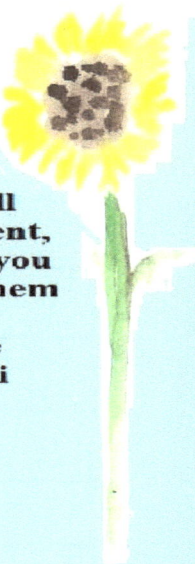

DATE:_____

JOURNAL: _____
_____
_____
_____
_____

Our Special Moments

Date: _____   Time: _____   Location: _____

Journal: _____

_____

_____

_____

_____

_____

_____

_____

_____

_____

_____

_____

Now that you are five and going on to six years old, a lot of new things are happening. You will start Kindergarten this year. You may lose a few front teeth. The tooth fairy will come by every time you lose a tooth. Stick the tooth under your pillow, before you go to sleep. In the morning, check to see if the tooth fairy left something special for you. Smile because you are a beautiful person.

I'm 5 years old

Date: _____

Journal: _____

_____

_____

_____

Our Special Moments

Date: _____   **Time:** _____   **Location:** _____

Journal: _____

_____

_____

_____

_____

_____

_____

_____

_____

_____

_____

_____

I'm here for you!

It's ok

Best friends forever

After the age of six, you will have your groups of friends at school, home and outside that you love to play with. You may meet your life long best friend, who you know you can always count on. You may begin to experience peer pressure, from now until your college years. Peer pressure is when you are asked to do something, yet inside, you don't feel good about it. When you feel this and need help, on what to do, come ask Mama or Papa or someone you feel safe. It is okay not to do something that you don't feel good about. At times, you may need to say "NO" to friends. You are terrific!

DATE: _____

JOURNAL: _____
_____
_____
_____
_____

Our Special Moments

Date: _____   **Time:** _____   **Location:** _____

Journal: _____

_____

_____

_____

_____

_____

_____

_____

_____

_____

_____

_____

Between eight and sixteen years old, you will have one or two spiritual rites of passage. Like First Communion and Confirmation or others may be Bar mitzvah. These rites of passage are special moments and you will learn about a higher being of God. Religion is to believe in the unseen, such as God. He loves you, gives you a lot of hugs and kisses like I do. XOXO I love you so.

DATE: _____

JOURNAL: _____
_____
_____
_____
_____

Our Special Moments

Date: _____ **Time:** _____ **Location:** _____

Journal: _____

_____

_____

_____

_____

_____

_____

_____

_____

_____

_____

_____

The beauty of life's changes

Around age 10-12 years old, sweetie, your body will start to change. This is normal. This is a sign that you are growing up. We will talk more about it, and most likely have a Mommy and me weekend to talk about the changes and things that you will experience and feel. We can talk about the "the birds and the bees." You can ask us anything you want. I love you.

DATE: _____

JOURNAL: _____
_____
_____
_____
_____

Our Special Moments

Date: _____   **Time:** _____   **Location:** _____

Journal: _____

_____

_____

_____

_____

_____

_____

_____

_____

_____

_____

_____

At 14 years old, you are going into your freshman year of high school. There are some changes. Enjoy four years of high school. It goes by fast. Homework comes first, and I hope you participate in extra curricular activities and some school dances. This is a time that you might be interested in dating and experience more peer pressure. I encourage you to wait to have a "boyfriend-girlfriend," because you still have a lot of time for that. Don't feel pressured, that you "have to" do what your friends might be doing, such as drugs or alcohol, etc. Have fun with your friends. My ears are open to listen to the feelings and concerns that you might have. If you feel that you cannot share them with Mom or Dad, please share them with someone you feel safe with and you trust that will give you good advice. I understand and love you.

DATE: _____

JOURNAL: _____
_____
_____
_____
_____
_____

Our Special Moments

Date: _____ Time: _____ Location: _____

Journal: _____
_____
_____
_____
_____
_____
_____
_____
_____
_____
_____
_____

Happy Sweet 16, Sweetie! We will plan your 16th birthday bash together. Oh my, you are two years away from entering college. Where has the time gone? And, this means Mama is getting older. I appreciate and thank God that I have you in my life. You are such a beautiful person. I cherish all the moments we have together. They are imprinted in my mind. If you are ready, we will practice driving a car. Don't forget to buckle your safety belt and keep your eyes on the road. Please let pedestrians cross before you drive on. Love always, your Mama.

DATE: _____

JOURNAL: _____
_____
_____
_____

Our Special Moments

Date: _____   Time: _____   Location: _____

Journal: _____

_____

_____

_____

_____

_____

_____

_____

_____

_____

_____

At 18 years old, you will have many changes and decisions to make. It is also an exciting time of your life. You are graduating from high school, getting ready for college, saying goodbye to some friends, making new friends, and developing your own unique identity. Knowing who you are and what your career interest is, may take a few years. This is the time to learn new things, that you haven't experienced while you were growing up. But don't rush it!

You might be dating and believe that this person may be "the one." I encourage you to take things slow and not be wrapped into one person. Don't let anyone make you feel pressured to "give yourself" to them. If you are not ready, it is okay to say "No." It is a beautiful thing, when you are with the right person. I wish you the best of luck with your future; in whatever path you choose to take. I will always be in your heart wherever you go Dear. Go as far as your abilities will take you and be passionate with everything you do. I love you dearly.

DATE: _____

JOURNAL: _____
_____
_____
_____
_____

Our Special Moments

Date: _____   **Time:** _____   **Location:** _____

Journal: _____

_____

_____

_____

_____

_____

_____

_____

_____

_____

_____

_____

As you read this page, you have graduated from college and have a career.

Perhaps you have found your life partner and are ready to marry. On your wedding day, my love, I can imagine how spectacular and amazing you will look – a breath of fresh air that sparkles like diamonds!

My wish is that your spouse will treasure you always, as I have.

I love you so much

Our Special Moments

Date: _____ Time: _____ Location: _____

Journal: _____

_____

_____

_____

_____

_____

_____

_____

_____

_____

_____

My Darling
Maybe you haven't met
your true love yet. Be patient.
Perhaps you want to follow
a career. You may choose
not to marry.
    At sometime in the
future you may choose
to adopt a child or
have a child on your own.
        I support your
decision.   Love always,
                    mama

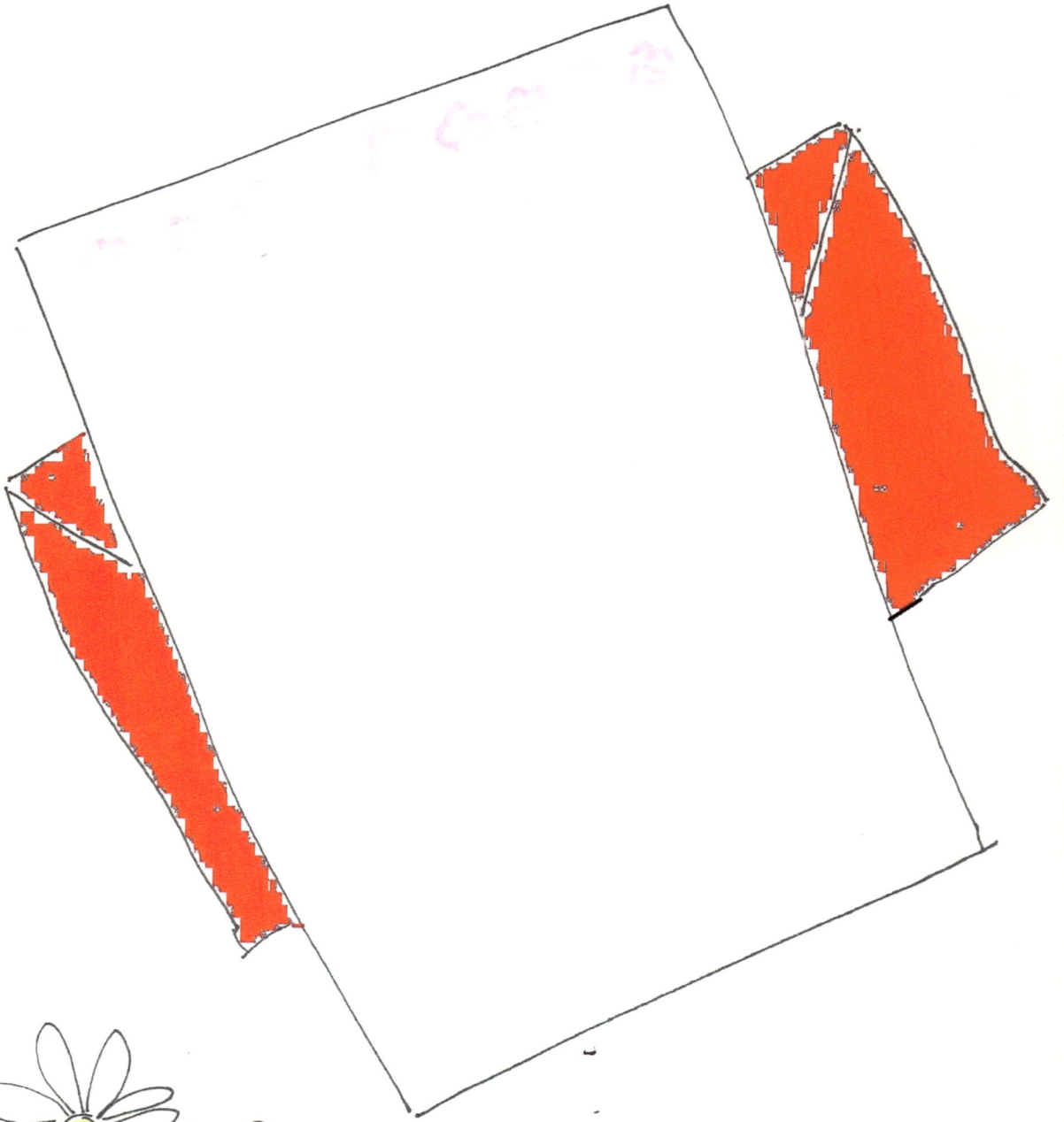

All lives have endings. My dear, if I'm still around at this time of your life, I want you to know what my wishes are. This will help you to not have to make difficult decisions. You still have your life to live.

My wish is to be in a nursing home that will take care of me. Whenever you have time from your busy schedule, come visit and have lunch or dinner with me. I don't expect you to come every day. You should take good care of yourself and be happy. When I pass away, just know that we will eventually meet again, and I will always be looking down upon you. You are a precious gem; keep smiling, because I always love you.

Our Special Moments

Date: _____   **Time:** _____   **Location:** _____

Journal: _____

_____

_____

_____

_____

_____

_____

_____

_____

_____

_____

_____

Our Special Moments

Date: _____ **Time:** _____ **Location:** _____

Journal: _____

_____

_____

_____

_____

_____

_____

_____

_____

_____

_____

_____

Date: _____   **Time:** _____   **Location:** _____

Journal: _____

_____

_____

_____

_____

_____

_____

_____

_____

_____

_____

_____

connections
of L♡VE

www.ingramcontent.com/pod-product-compliance
Lightning Source LLC
Chambersburg PA
CBHW060814090426
42737CB00002B/66